Antonio

A PREPARATION FOR FIRST EUCHARIST

CALLED TO HIS SUPPER

REVISED

Includes
Revised Order
of Mass
✝

JEANNINE TIMKO LEICHNER
ILLUSTRATED BY KEVIN DAVIDSON

Our Sunday Visitor Publishing Division
Our Sunday Visitor, Inc.
Huntington, Indiana 46750

Nihil Obstat:
Rev. Michael Heintz
Censor Librorum

Imprimatur:
✠ John M. D'Arcy
Bishop of Fort Wayne-South Bend
May 14, 2007

Excerpts from the English translation for Lectionary for Mass © 1969,1981,1997,
International Committee on English in the Liturgy, Inc. (ICEL). Excerpts from the English
translation of the *Roman Missal* © 2010, International Committee
on English in the Liturgy, Inc. All rights reserved.

Our Sunday Visitor Publishing Division
Our Sunday Visitor, Inc.
200 Noll Plaza
Huntington, IN 46750

ISBN: 978-1-59276-299-6 (Inventory No. X389)

Interior design by Rebecca J. Heaston
Cover art by Kevin Davidson

PRINTED IN THE UNITED STATES OF AMERICA

My heartfelt thanks to my husband, Gene,
and my friend, Anne Styles, for their encouragement,
help, and support.

If you have ever been to Mass and wished you could receive Holy Communion with everyone else, this book is for <u>you!</u>

One day, when you were small, your family brought you to Church to be baptized.

They wanted to share their faith in Jesus with you.

Draw a picture of your family.

The day you received the Sacrament of Baptism was a special day in your life.

On the day you were baptized, God's love poured over you like w_____.

You were freed from sin and filled with a new kind of l_____ in Jesus and the Holy Spirit.

Being baptized is like being born again!

MY BAPTISM

My name is _____

I was baptized on _____

at _____ Church

in_____

My godparents are _____

_____

3

When you were baptized you became a **CHILD** of **GOD** and a part of God's special family called the **CHURCH**.

Belonging to God's family is **GREAT!**

4

Baptism planted the seed of God's love in your heart so that you could grow to be like Jesus.

Tell them to fill the jars with w_____.

Jesus helped people who were in trouble.

I am like Jesus when I

_____

_____

_____

Baptism was the beginning of your life as a C_____ Christian.

C	H	R	I	S	T	I	A	N	S	X	F	O	L	L	O	W
X	T	H	E	X	W	A	Y	X	O	F	X	J	E	S	U	S

5

Sunday is a very special day for Catholic Christians. On Sunday we come together to celebrate the MASS

The Mass is our family CELEBRATION

More than anything else the Mass is a celebration of L♥VE.

Think about the last time you went to Mass.

What did you see?
What did you hear?
What did you do?

I like it when _____

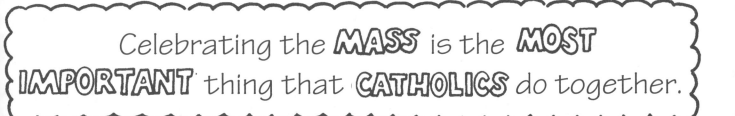

Celebrating the **MASS** is the **MOST** **IMPORTANT** thing that **CATHOLICS** do together.

When we gather together to celebrate the Mass, **JESUS** is with us!

Whenever people gather in my name, I will be with them.

Matthew 18:20

Coming together with Jesus gives us **JOY.**

We begin our celebration by making the sign of the cross. The sign of the ✝ reminds us of Jesus' great ♡ for us.

In the name of the F_____
and of the S_____ and of the
H_____ S_____.
Amen.

Then we ask God
to forgive us for
the times we
failed to love as
Jesus did.

Lord, have _____.
Christ, have _____.
Lord, have _____.

THE LORD IS KIND AND MERCIFUL

With joyful hearts we praise and thank God for his goodness by singing

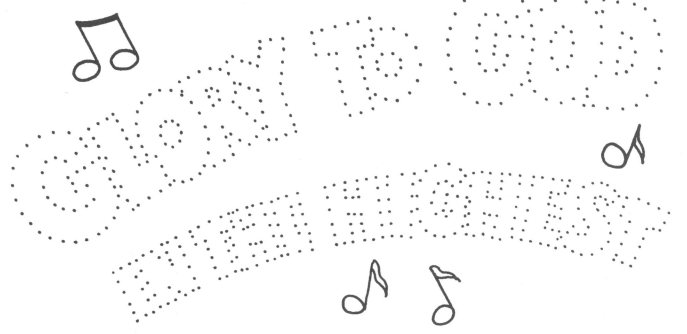

GLORY TO GOD IN THE HIGHEST

Draw a picture of one of the wonderful gifts that God has created.

People long ago loved to listen to Jesus.

He taught them how to l_____ God and others.

At Mass, we hear Jesus speaking to us in readings from the holy B_____.

He teaches u__ how to l_____ God and others.

JESUS' WORDS ARE GOD'S WORDS

Jesus' words are important for us. We need to listen to them carefully, to let them sink into our hearts ♡ ♡ ♡ and become part of our lives.

The priest helps us understand what Jesus is saying to us in the readings. This is called the h_____.

The readings tell us many things.
They tell us how much God l_____ us,
they help us know what to d___,
they comfort us when we are
s_____ or worried
and <u>much more</u>!

The readings also help us think of people who need our prayers. We pray for them, and for ourselves, at the Prayer of the Faithful.

Who would you like to pray for?

♡ _____

♡ _____

♡ _____

♡ _____

♡ _____

Lord, hear our prayer.

Happy are you who hear the Word of GOD and keep it!

Can You Find Help?

A sick person needs

A person who is hungry needs

Someone who is lost needs

A person who is hurt needs

A lonely person needs a

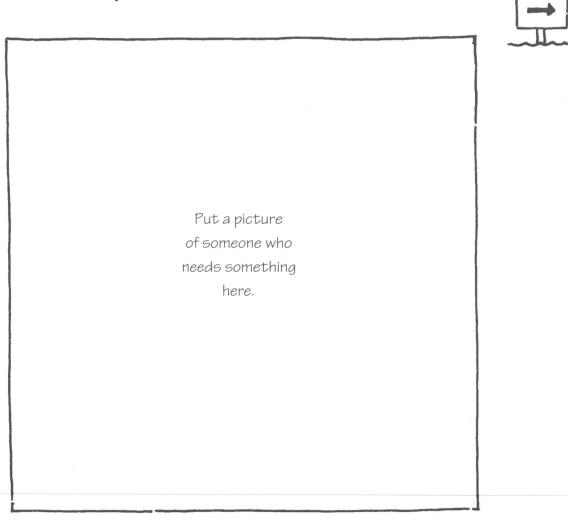

Put a picture
of someone who
needs something
here.

What does the person in the picture need?

_____

Who could help? _____

JESUS AND THE PEOPLE WHO NEEDED HIM

One day Jesus and his disciples went to a quiet place to rest. A large crowd followed them.

When Jesus saw the people, they reminded him of sheep without a shepherd, and he began to teach them.

The people loved to listen to Jesus. They stayed with him a long time.

When it grew late, Jesus' disciples thought the people might be getting hungry. They talked to Jesus and said he should send the people away, so they could get some food in the villages nearby.

Jesus looked at his disciples. He told them that they should give the people something to eat.

The disciples didn't know what to do. They only had five loaves of bread and two little fish. They were sure that would never be enough for so many people.

Jesus had the people sit down on the grass. Then he took the five loaves and two fish into his hands and looked up to heaven.

He blessed them,
broke them,
and gave them
to his disciples to
give to the people.

Everyone ate until they were full.

When they were finished, Jesus told his disciples to collect the pieces that were left over. They filled _____ baskets!

Mark 6:34-44

Imagine that you were one of the people that Jesus fed that day.

How did you feel?
What did you do?
What did you tell your friends about Jesus when you went home?

_____

_____

_____

Find the Right Words

l	o	v	e	d	s
t	z	o	f	e	d
u	d	m	j	x	g
k	h	e	a	r	v
c	y	w	n	q	e
n	e	e	d	e	d

1. Many people came to see and h_____ Jesus.

2. Jesus l_____ the people.

3. He taught them and he f____ them.

4. He gave them what they n_____.

A Prayer
The hand of the Lord feeds us.
He answers all our needs.

We are like the people who came to Jesus.
We need to be <u>taught</u> and we need to be <u>fed</u>.

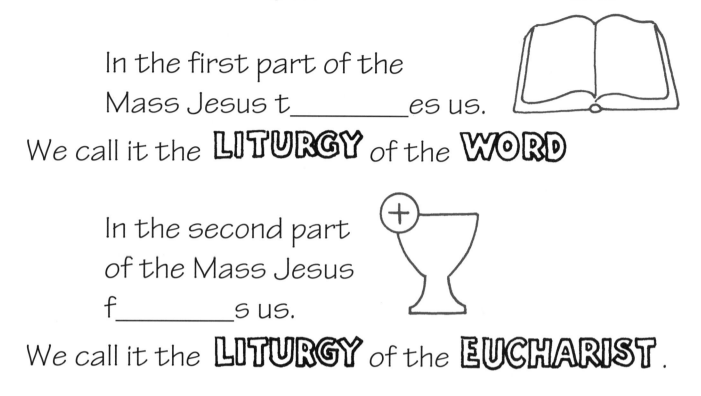

In the first part of the
Mass Jesus t_____es us.
We call it the **LITURGY** of the **WORD**

In the second part
of the Mass Jesus
f_____s us.
We call it the **LITURGY** of the **EUCHARIST**.

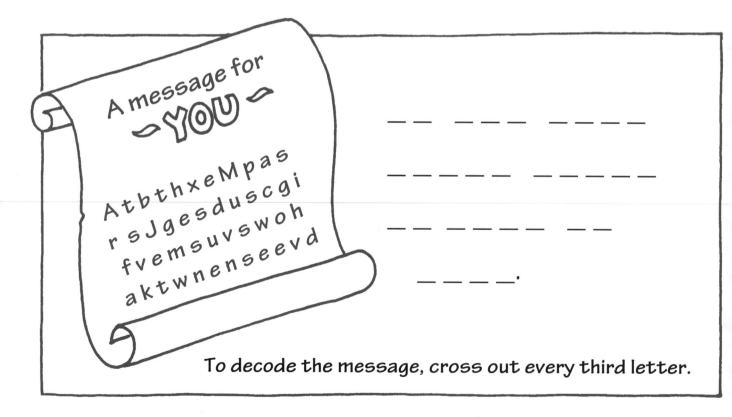

A message for
~ **YOU** ~

AtbthxeMpas
rsJgesduscgi
fvemsuvswoh
aktwnenseevd

____ ____ ____ ____

____ ____ ____ ____

____ ____ ____ __

____ ____.

To decode the message, cross out every third letter.

FAMILY MEALS ARE SPECIAL TIMES

When my family eats together we

sing	talk	run	listen
eat	laugh	sleep	draw
pray	jump	smile	share

We like to eat together because _____

_____.

Sometimes when we
are hungry we eat by
ourselves,

but eating with
family or friends is nicer than eating alone.

Eating together shows
that we c_____ for one another.
Who do you like to eat with?

_____

22

Jesus liked to eat with his friends and his Apostles. They were like his family.

Sometimes Jesus ate with people who had sinned and people that no one else liked.

Why do you think he did that?

_____

Do you ever eat with someone who is all alone?

_____

SCRAMBLED WORDS

Sharing like food is sharing love

Sharing food is like sharing love.

At the Liturgy of the Eucharist, Jesus invites us to come to his table.

He loves us and wants to share himself with us in a holy meal.

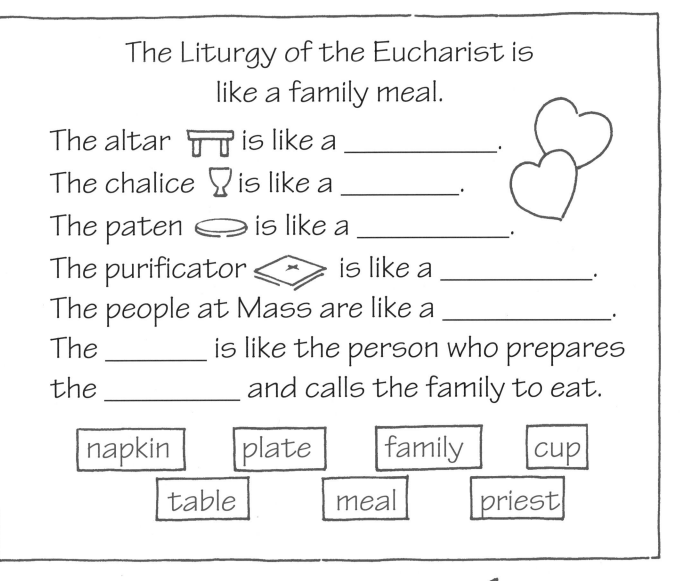

The Liturgy of the Eucharist is
like a family meal.

The altar ⊓ is like a _____.

The chalice ♈ is like a _____.

The paten ⬯ is like a _____.

The purificator ⬦ is like a _____.

The people at Mass are like a _____.

The _____ is like the person who prepares

the _____ and calls the family to eat.

| napkin | plate | family | cup |

| table | meal | priest |

Gather, gather 'round his table.
He loves us, he loves us.
Listen to him teach us,
Share the food he gives us.
He is Lord! He is Lord!

The food we use at the Liturgy of the Eucharist is **BREAD** and **WINE** .

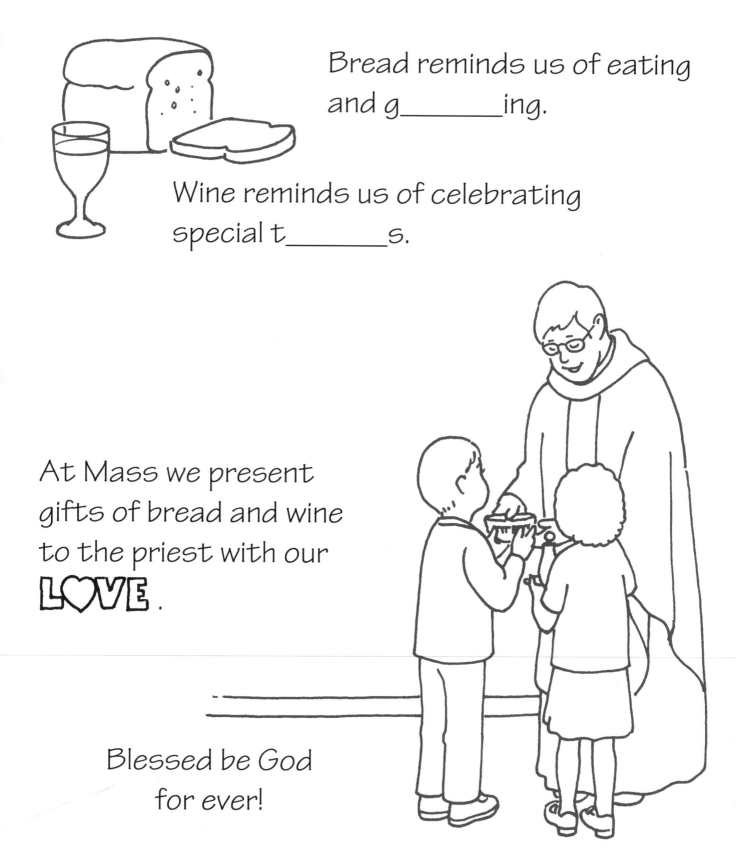

Bread reminds us of eating and g_____ing.

Wine reminds us of celebrating special t_____s.

At Mass we present gifts of bread and wine to the priest with our **LOVE** .

Blessed be God for ever!

In our prayers we ask God
to take our gifts and make
them holy so that they will
become the

EUCHARIST

The Eucharist will become our food.

Some meals are more important than others.
They help us celebrate something special.

On Thanksgiving, we
celebrate_____

_____.

At a birthday dinner, we
celebrate _____

_____.

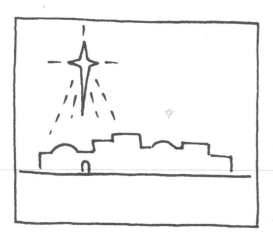

At Christmas dinner, we
celebrate _____

_____.

When we celebrate,
we _____.

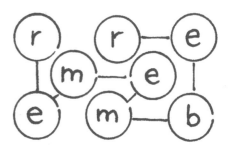

Jesus ate many ordinary meals with his Apostles, but each year they had a special meal together. It was called Passover.

Celebrating Passover helped them remember God's goodness.

Jesus and his Apostles celebrated a Passover meal the night before he died. It was his Last Supper.

At the Last Supper Jesus thought about his Apostles. He wanted to be near them always.

He also thought about everyone who would ever live. He knew that soon he would give his life to save all people.

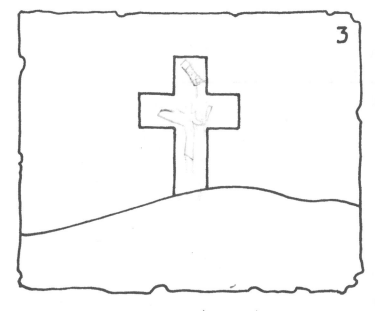

At the Last Supper, Jesus took a piece of bread, blessed it, broke it, and gave it to his Apostles. He said, "Take and eat. This is my body."

Later he took a cup of wine, blessed it, and gave it to his Apostles. He said, "Take and drink. This is my blood."

Then he said,
"Do this
in memory
of me."

When the Apostles ate the bread and drank the wine that Jesus gave them, they were closer to him than ever before.

Jesus gave himself to his Apostles in the bread and wine to show them how much he loved them.

He wanted to be with them always.

At the Last Supper, Jesus gave us the Eucharist.

The next day, Jesus gave his life for us on the cross.

The E_____ and the c_____ tell us how much Jesus loves us.

JESUS is the SAVIOR of the WORLD

After Jesus died, he rose to new life! His friends thought about him often and remembered what he said at the L_____ S_____.

And so they took b_____ and w_____ and did what Jesus had done.

When they remembered Jesus in this way, they felt his l_____ and they knew he was w_____ them.

We remember Jesus in the same way at the Liturgy of the Eucharist.

The priest takes a piece
of bread and says,
"Take and eat,
all of you,

_____ __ __ _____.

Then he takes a cup
of wine and says,
"Take and drink,
all of you,

_____ __ __ _____.

Do this in memory of me.

When the priest does what Jesus did at the Last Supper, our gifts of bread and wine are changed through the power of the Holy Spirit.

THE BREAD AND WINE BECOME JESUS' BODY AND BLOOD.

Jesus is with us in a wonderful and mysterious new way that we call the Eucharist.

I am t_e living b_ead th_t c_me down f_om hea_en.

John 6:51

The Eucharist is the Sacrament of Jesus' body and blood.

The Eucharist looks and tastes like bread and wine, but it is truly Jesus.

We believe that the Eucharist is Jesus' body and blood because we believe that what Jesus said is true.

We have **FAITH IN JESUS!**

At the Liturgy of the Eucharist, Jesus' sacrifice of himself on the cross becomes present now.

We proclaim the mystery of faith:
    When we eat this B_____ and drink this
        C___, we proclaim you Death, O Lord,
            until you c_____ again.

At the Liturgy of the Eucharist we offer Jesus'
b_____ and b_____ to God in joyful praise
and thanksgiving.

Through him, with him, and in him, O God, almighty
Father, in the unity of the Holy Spirit, all glory and
honor is yours, for ever and ever.

Jesus loves us as much as he loved his Apostles.
At Mass, he gives himself to us in Holy

The word Comm<u>union</u> tells us that when we receive
the Eucharist we are <u>united</u> with Jesus!

We are as close to him as we can be.

We **SHARE** his **LIFE** and **LOVE**!

I am the v_____,
you are the br_____.
Joined to me you will
do much g_____.

John 15:5

40

Celebrating the Eucharist is . . .

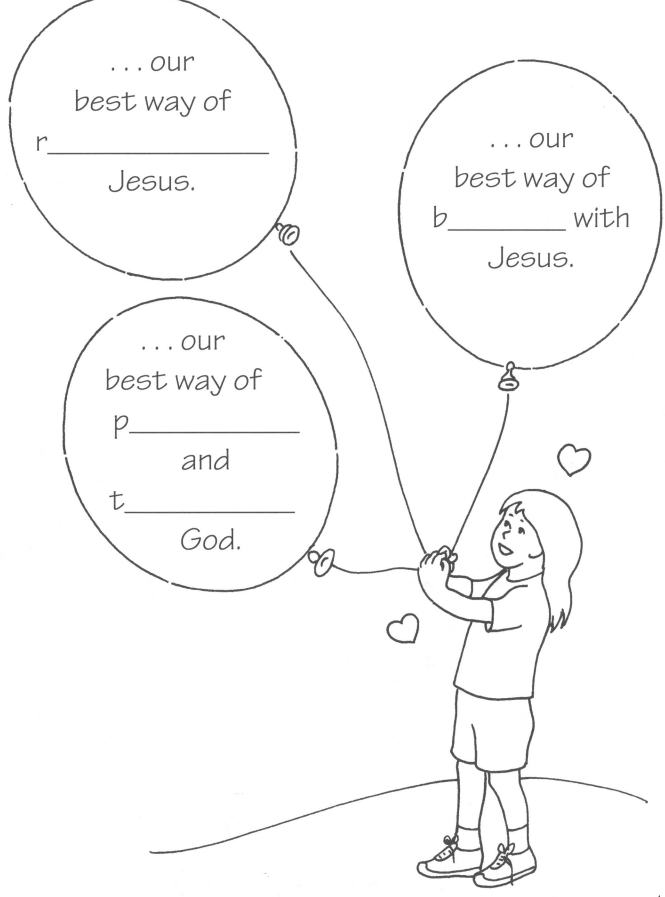

. . . our best way of r_____ Jesus.

. . . our best way of b_____ with Jesus.

. . . our best way of p_____ and t_____ God.

Before we receive Holy Communion, we pray the Our Father together.

Our Father,
who art in _____,
hallowed be thy _____;
thy kingdom come, thy will be done
on _____ as it is in _____.
Give us this _____ our daily _____;
and _____ us our trespasses
as we _____ those who trespass
against us.
And lead us ____ into
temptation, but _____
us from evil.

```
x  x  d  e  l  i  v  e  r
b  r  e  a  d  x  d  a  y
x  f  o  r  g  i  v  e  x
x  n  o  t  x  n  a  m  e
x  x  x  h  e  a  v  e  n
```

We also offer each other a sign of peace to prepare our hearts to receive Jesus in Holy Communion.

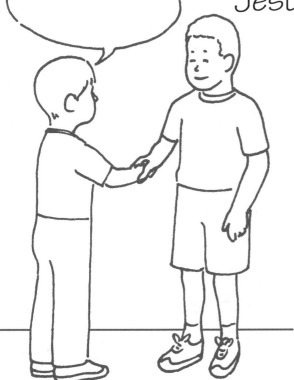

When we offer someone a sign of peace it means that we _____ _____.

As the priest breaks the b_____ and prepares our holy m_____, we pray and sing.

"Lamb of God, you take away the s____ of the world, have m_____ on us. . . ."

BLESSED ARE THOSE CALLED TO THE SUPPER OF THE LAMB.

Lord, I am not worthy that you should enter under my roof, but only say the word and my soul shall be healed.

When the priest gives us Holy Communion, he says, "The body of C_____." We answer, "A_____," because we know this is Jesus.

Communion time is a **JOYFUL** time! We sing about the wonderful gift of Jesus in the Eucharist.

Singing together reminds us that everyone who shares this holy meal is <u>united in love</u>.

JESUS MAKES US ONE FAMILY

When we receive Holy Communion, we spend some quiet time with Jesus.

Imagine that you have just received Jesus in the Eucharist. What would you say to him to welcome him into your heart? How would you like him to help you?

My Communion Prayer

_____

_____

_____

_____

_____

When the Mass is over, the priest blesses us and says, "Go in p_____."
We answer, "T_____ be to G_____."

We have come together to remember Jesus' ♡ for us and he has made our ♡ for one another grow stronger.

When we leave the celebration of the Eucharist,
Jesus wants us to share his ♡ with everyone!
He wants us to be his **BODY** in the world.

Draw a picture of how you could share Jesus' love with someone.

Jesus wants us, big and small,
To give his love to one and a____.
By what we say and what we do
We let them know he loves
them, t____.

Remembering What We Learned

1. The Mass is our f_____ celebration.

2. When we come together to celebrate the Mass, J_____ is with us.

3. At Mass, Jesus speaks to us through the r_____ and in the h_____.

4. When the priest does what Jesus did at the L_____ S_____, the bread and wine become Jesus' b_____ and b_____.

5. At Mass, we o_____ Jesus' body and blood to God with our love.

6. When we receive Holy C_____, we receive Jesus.

7. Sharing the E_____ unites us with Jesus and with one another.

8. When our celebration is over, Jesus wants us to take his l_____ wherever we go.

Do you remember the story of the people who needed Jesus?

The day after Jesus fed the people they came back to him. They wanted more food.

Jesus told them he would give them a new kind of food, food that would last.

When the people asked Jesus how they could get this new food he said,

"I am the

BREAD of LIFE.
Anyone who eats this bread
will live for ever."

When Jesus called himself the Bread of Life, he was really talking about the Eucharist.

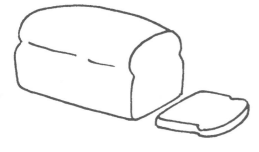

He wanted us to know that the Eucharist is as important for us to eat as b_____ is.

The Eucharist is food that helps us g_____ in our ♡ for God and other people.

The Eucharist is food that will lead us to everlasting l_____.

ATHEMEUCHARISTOYIS

THEDBREADNOFCLIFEMP

Before long, you will celebrate your first Holy Communion.

I will receive my first Holy Communion on

_____

at _____ o'clock Mass

at_____

Church.

The day that you receive Jesus, the Bread of Life, for the first time will be one of the special days of your life.

LORD, GIVE US THIS BREAD ALWAYS

When you receive your first Holy Communion,
Jesus will wrap you in his love.

You are God's precious
child and Jesus is your
b_____ friend!

You can open your heart
to Jesus.
He will always l_____ to
you and understand.

He will give you what you
n_____ and fill you with
peace and joy.

I LOVE YOU JESUS

After you receive your First Holy Communion, you can receive Communion <u>every Sunday</u> when you celebrate the Mass with God's family.

Hurray for _____!

The Eucharist is f_____ for the rest of your life!

Every time you share the Eucharist,

JESUS WILL BE WITH YOU

He will help the love inside you g_____ more and more like h___ love.

Your first Holy Communion day will be one of the special days of your life, and the <u>beginning of many more</u> to come!

Blessed are those called to the supper of the Lamb.

I CONFESS

I confess to almighty God,
and to you my brothers and sisters,
that I have greatly sinned
   in my thoughts
   and in my words,
   in what I have done
   and in what I have failed to do,
through my fault,
through my fault,
through my most grievous fault;
therefore I ask blessed Mary ever-Virgin,
all the Angels and Saints,
and you, my brothers and sisters,
to pray for me to the Lord our God.

Lord, have mercy. Christ, have mercy. Lord, have mercy.

THE GLORIA

Glory to God in the highest,
and on earth peace to people of good will.

We praise you, we bless you, we adore you, we glorify
you, we give you thanks for your great glory,
Lord God, heavenly King, O God, almighty Father.

Lord Jesus Christ, Only Begotten Son,
Lord God, Lamb of God, Son of the Father,
you take away the sins of the world, have mercy
on us; you take away the sins of the world, receive
our prayer; you are seated at the right hand of the
Father, have mercy on us.

For you alone are the Holy One,
   you alone are the Lord,
      you alone are the Most High,
         JESUS CHRIST,
      with the Holy Spirit,
   in the glory of God the Father. Amen.

Holy, holy, holy Lord,
God of hosts.
        Heaven
        and
        earth
        are full of your glory.

Hosanna in the highest.

Blessed is he
        who comes in the
        name of the Lord.

Hosanna in the highest!

59

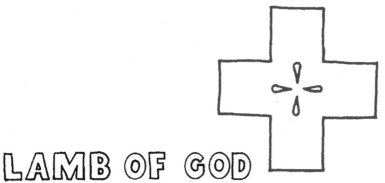

LAMB OF GOD

you take away the sins of the world:
have mercy on us.

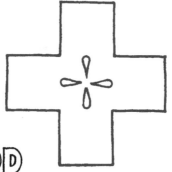

LAMB OF GOD

you take away the sins of the world:
have mercy on us.

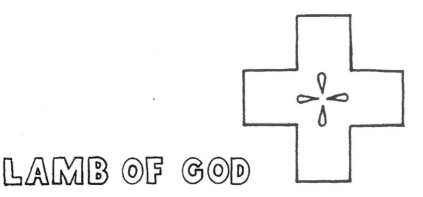

LAMB OF GOD

you take away the sins of the world:
grant us peace.